Paul Revere's Ride

Henry Wadsworth Longfellow

Illustrated by John Fairbridge

*In the late 1700s, America was struggling
to gain independence from Britain.
Paul Revere was one man who wanted
that struggle to succeed — and on April 18,
1775, he galloped through the night
to warn the people of Massachusetts
that British troops were approaching.
Here is how Henry Wadsworth Longfellow,
an American poet of the 1800s,
remembers Paul Revere's
famous midnight ride . . .*

Map and Glossary p. 32

Listen, my children, and you shall hear
 Of the midnight ride of Paul Revere
On the eighteenth of April, in Seventy-five;
 Hardly a man is now alive
Who remembers that famous day and year.

He said to his friend, "If the British march
 By land or sea from the town tonight,
Hang a lantern aloft in the belfry arch
 Of the North Church tower as a signal light.
One light if by land, or two if by sea;
 And I on the opposite shore will be,
Ready to ride and spread the alarm
 Through every Middlesex village and farm,
For the country folk to be up and to arm."

Then he said *Good night,* and with muffled oar
   Silently rowed to the Charlestown shore,
Just as the moon rose over the bay,
   Where swinging wide at her moorings lay
The Somerset, British man-o'-war;
   A phantom ship, with each mast and spar
Across the moon like a prison bar,
   And a huge black hulk, that was magnified
By its own reflection in the tide.

Meanwhile his friend, through alley and street,
  Wanders and watches with eager ears,
Till in silence around him he hears
  The muster of men at the barrack door,
The sound of drums, and the tramp of feet,
  And the measured tread of the grenadiers,
Marching down to their boats on the shore.

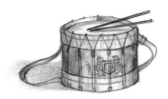

Then he climbed to the tower of the church,
    Up the wooden stairs, with stealthy tread,
To the belfry-chamber overhead,
    And startled the pigeons from their perch
On the somber rafters, that round him made
    Masses and moving shapes of shade —
Up the trembling ladder, steep and tall,
    To the highest window in the wall,
Where he paused to listen and look down
    A moment on the roofs of the town,
And the moonlight flowing over all.

Beneath, in the churchyard, lay the dead,
  In their night-encampment on the hill,
Wrapped in silence so deep and still
  That he could hear like a sentinel's tread,
The watchful night-wind, as it went
  Creeping along from tent to tent,
And seeming to whisper, "All is well!"

Then suddenly all his thoughts are bent
On a shadowy something far away,
Where the river widens to meet the bay —
A line of black that bends and floats
On the rising tide, like a bridge of boats.

Meanwhile, impatient to mount and ride,
  Booted and spurred, with a heavy stride
On the opposite shore walked Paul Revere.
  Now he patted his horse's side,
Now he gazed at the landscape far and near,
  Then, impetuous, stamped the earth,
And turned and tightened his saddle-girth.

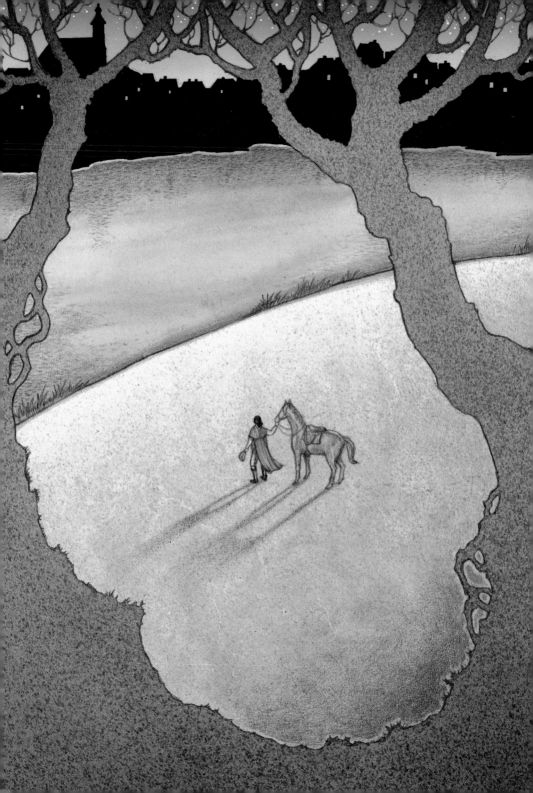

But mostly he watched with eager search
  The belfry-tower of the Old North Church,
As it rose above the graves on the hill,
  Lonely and spectral and somber and still,
And lo! as he looks, on the belfry's height
  A glimmer, and then a gleam of light!
He springs to the saddle, the bridle he turns,
  But lingers and gazes, till full on his sight
A second lamp in the belfry burns!

$\textbf{A}$ hurry of hoofs in a village street,
  A shape in the moonlight, a bulk in the dark,
And beneath, from the pebbles, in passing, a spark
  Struck out by a steed flying fearless and fleet;
That was all!

$\textbf{A}$nd yet, throughout the gloom and the light,
  The fate of a nation was riding that night;
And the spark struck out by that steed in flight,
  Kindled the land into flame with its heat.

He has left the village and mounted the steep,
    And beneath him: tranquil, broad, and deep,
Is the Mystic, meeting the ocean tides;
    And under the alders that skirt its edge,
Now soft on the sand, now loud on the ledge,
    Is heard the tramp of his steed as he rides.

It was twelve by the village clock
  When he crossed the bridge to Medford town.
He heard the crowing of the cock,
  And the barking of the farmer's dog,
And felt the damp of the river fog,
  That rises after the sun goes down.

It was one by the village clock,
  When he galloped into Lexington.
He saw the gilded weathercock
  Swim in the moonlight as he passed,
And the meetinghouse windows, blank and bare,
  Gazed at him with a spectral glare,
As if they already stood aghast
  At the bloody work they would look upon.

It was two by the village clock,
  When he came to the bridge in Concord town,
He heard the bleating of the flock,
  And the twitter of birds among the trees,
And felt the breath of the morning breeze
  Blowing over the meadows brown.
And one was safe and asleep in his bed
  Who at the bridge would be first to fall,
Who that day would be lying dead,
  Pierced by a British musket-ball.

You know the rest. In books you have read,
　　How the British Regulars fired and fled —
How the farmers gave them ball for ball,
　　From behind each fence and farmyard wall,
Chasing the redcoats down the lane,
　　Then crossing the fields to emerge again
Under the trees at the turn of the road,
　　And only pausing to fire and load.

So through the night rode Paul Revere;
  So through the night went his cry of alarm
To every Middlesex village and farm —
  A cry of defiance and not of fear,
A voice in the darkness, a knock at the door,
  And a word that shall echo for evermore!

For borne on the night-wind of the Past,
  Through all our history, to the last,
In the hour of darkness and peril and need
  The people will waken and listen to hear
The hurrying hoofbeats of that steed,
  And the midnight message of Paul Revere.

Map and Glossary

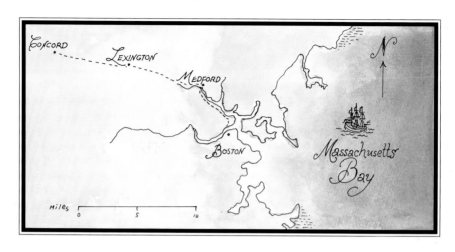

aghast — filled with horror

alder — a type of tree

aloft — up high

barrack — a building in which soldiers live

belfry — a tower for a bell

encampment — a place where people are camped

fleet — swift, quick

gilded — the color of gold

grenadiers — special soldiers who were chosen for their height and strength

impetuous — wanting to act quickly

moorings — the place where ships are tied up

musket — early form of rifle

musket ball — type of bullet

Mystic — Massachusetts seaport

peril — danger

redcoat — British soldier

saddle-girth — the strap that keeps a saddle on a horse

sentinel — a guard who stands watch

somber — dark and gloomy

spar — a large pole

spectral — like a ghost

steed — a horse for riding

tranquil — quiet and peaceful

weathercock — device to show which way the wind blows